COOL
MAKERSPACE
GADGETS & GIZMOS

MOVE IT!
PROJECTS YOU CAN DRIVE, FLY, AND ROLL

Christa Schneider

Checkerboard
Library

An Imprint of Abdo Publishing
abdopublishing.com

abdopublishing.com

Published by Abdo Publishing, a division of ABDO, PO Box 398166, Minneapolis, Minnesota 55439. Copyright © 2018 by Abdo Consulting Group, Inc. International copyrights reserved in all countries. No part of this book may be reproduced in any form without written permission from the publisher. Checkerboard Library™ is a trademark and logo of Abdo Publishing.

Printed in the United States of America, North Mankato, Minnesota
102017
012018

THIS BOOK CONTAINS
RECYCLED MATERIALS

Design: Sarah DeYoung, Mighty Media, Inc.
Production: Mighty Media, Inc.
Editor: Liz Salzmann
Cover Photographs: Mighty Media, Inc.; Shutterstock
Interior Photographs: iStockphoto; Mighty Media, Inc.; Shutterstock

The following manufacturers/names appearing in this book are trademarks: Alltrade®, Artist's Loft™, Cubelets®, Duracell®, Elenco®, K'NEX®, LEGO®, littleBits™, Snap Circuits®

Publisher's Cataloging-in-Publication Data
Names: Schneider, Christa, author.
Title: Move it! projects you can drive, fly, and roll / by Christa
   Schneider.
Other titles: Projects you can drive, fly, and roll
Description: Minneapolis, Minnesota : Abdo Publishing, 2018. I
   Series: Cool makerspace gadgets & gizmos I Includes online
   resources and index.
Identifiers: LCCN 2017944034 I ISBN 9781532112546 (lib.bdg.) I
   ISBN 9781614799962 (ebook)
Subjects: LCSH: Inventions--Juvenile literature. I Creative ability
   in science--Juvenile literature. I Handicraft--Juvenile literature. I
   Makerspaces--Juvenile literature.
Classification: DDC 600--dc23
LC record available at https://lccn.loc.gov/2017944034

TO ADULT HELPERS

This is your chance to assist a young maker as they develop new skills, gain confidence, and make cool things! These activities are designed to help children create projects in makerspaces. Children may need more assistance for some activities than others. Be there to offer guidance when they need it. Encourage them to do as much as they can on their own. Be a cheerleader for their creativity.

Before getting started, remember to lay down ground rules for using tools and supplies and for cleaning up. There should always be adult supervision when using a hot or sharp tool.

SAFETY SYMBOLS

Some projects in this book require the use of hot or sharp tools. That means you'll need some adult help for these projects. Determine whether you'll need help on a project by looking for these safety symbols.

HOT!
This project requires the use of a hot tool.

SHARP!
This project requires the use of a sharp tool.

CONTENTS

What's a
MAKERSPACE?

Imagine a space buzzing with energy. All around you, marvelous makers and up-and-coming **engineers** are building cool creations. Welcome to a makerspace!

Makerspaces are areas where people come together to create. They are the perfect areas to create amazing projects that move! Makerspaces are equipped with all kinds of materials and tools. But a maker's most important tool is his or her imagination. Makers dream up brand-new projects that drive, fly, and roll. They find ways to put new twists on existing projects. To do this, makers need to be creative problem solvers. Are you ready to become a maker?

BEFORE YOU GET STARTED

GET PERMISSION

Ask an adult for **permission** to use the makerspace and materials before starting any project.

BE RESPECTFUL

Share tools and supplies with other makers. When you're done with a tool, put it back so others can use it.

MAKE A PLAN

Read through the instructions and gather all your supplies ahead of time. Keep them organized as you create!

BE SAFE

Working with electricity can be **dangerous**, so be careful! Keep your power source switched off when connecting wires. Prevent short circuits. Ask an adult for help when you need it.

WHAT CREATES MOTION?

Energy creates motion. Two main kinds of energy are potential energy and kinetic energy. Potential energy is energy stored in an object. When the object moves, it has kinetic energy. For example, when you stretch a rubber band, it gains potential energy. When you let go of the rubber band, kinetic energy causes it to shoot across the room.

Electricity is another kind of energy that can create motion. When a motor is connected to an electric circuit, it moves. Then, whatever object the motor is connected to moves too. There are many products and materials you can use to build amazing moving **gadgets** and gizmos.

K'NEX & LEGOS

K'NEX and LEGOs are two products that are perfect for makerspaces. Both feature plastic pieces of many shapes and sizes. The pieces fit together to create structures. LEGO Technics are more advanced LEGOs. These kits include rods, gears, and other types of parts. Just add your imagination!

ELECTRONIC KITS

One way to make a structure move is with an electric circuit. Products such as Cubelets, Snap Circuits, and littleBits make building electric circuits easy and safe. These products are sold in kits. The kits include motors, lights, wires, and other materials used to create different kinds of circuits. Many of these materials can be used with K'NEX and LEGO parts. Use these products together to make structures that roll, fly, zoom, and glide!

SUPPLIES

Here are some of the materials and tools used for the projects in this book. If your makerspace doesn't have what you need, don't worry! Find different supplies to substitute for the missing materials. Or modify the project to fit the supplies you have. Be creative!

Cubelets Six Kit

K'NEX clip connectors

K'NEX connectors

K'NEX rods

K'NEX spacers

K'NEX 375 Piece Deluxe Building Set

K'NEX wheels

LEGO basic bricks

LEGO bushings for cross axles

LEGO cross axles

LEGO double conical wheels

LEGO plates

LEGO Technic angled beam & bricks with holes

LEGO wheels

littleBits Gizmos
& Gadgets Kit

needle-nose
pliers

9-volt
battery

Snap Circuits Build
Over 300 Exciting
Projects Kit

DESIGN TIP

It's okay to make mistakes when building moving structures. Many of the materials can be taken apart and reused. So, if you're not happy with the way something works or looks, just try again! You could also start by drawing what you want to build. Then you'll have a plan to follow.

CIRCUIT FIXES

Products such as Snap Circuits and Cubelets make building circuits easier. But electric circuits can still be tricky. It's important to connect batteries, wires, and other parts correctly. If something doesn't work, check the connections. You might need to move a wire to a different connector or turn something around.

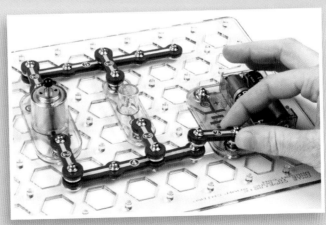

STEAMROLLER

Level the playing field with this heavy-duty machine!

1. Cut a 3⅛-inch (8 cm) piece off the toilet paper tube.

2. Cover your work surface with newspaper. Paint the outside of the tube piece black. Let the paint dry.

❸ Put a tan clip connector at the end of a red rod. The tab should point toward the end of the rod.

❹ Put a small wheel on the rod. Slide it next to the clip connector.

❺ Put the toilet paper tube piece on the rod. Put the other small wheel on the rod. Put a tan clip connector on the rod. Make sure the clip's tab points toward the end of the rod.

6. Push the clips snugly against the wheels to keep the toilet paper tube in place. This is the roller.

7. Connect a green rod and a white rod to a light gray connector. Connect a yellow connector to the green rod. Connect another green rod to the top of the yellow connector.

Continued on the next page.

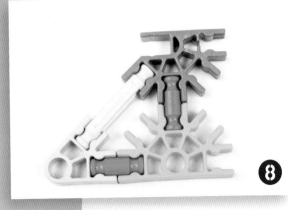

8 Attach a dark gray connector to the green rod and white rod. This is a front side **panel**.

9. Repeat steps 7 and 8 to create a second front side panel.

10 Put one end of the roller's red rod through the round hole in the corner of one front side panel. The tab of the tan clip connector should go into the hole next to the green rod. Attach the other front side panel to the other end of the roller.

11. Connect another red rod to the dark gray connectors.

12 Connect two blue rods to opposite sides of a white connector. Connect the other ends of the blue rods to the bottom slots of the yellow connectors. Make sure the white connector is upright. Set the roller aside.

13. Connect a blue rod to a white connector. Attach a yellow rod to the white connector two slots from the blue rod. Attach an end slot of a red connector to the top of the yellow rod.

14. Connect a white rod to the other end slot of the red connector. The white rod should point the same direction as the blue rod. This is a back support.

15. Repeat steps 13 and 14 to create a second back support.

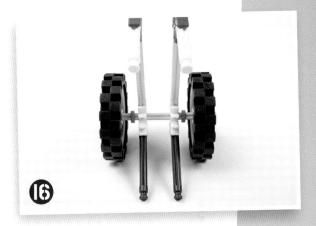

16 Hold the back supports so they are facing the same way. Put a yellow rod through the white connectors. Put a blue spacer and a large wheel on each end of the yellow rod.

17. Put a tan clip connector on each end of the yellow rod. Each clip's tab should go into the hole next to the wheel's center hole. Connect an orange connector to the white rods on the back supports.

18 Connect the back supports' blue rods to the white connector on the roller.

19 Use three white rods and four red connectors to complete three sides of a square. Attach the unconnected red connectors to the upright yellow rods. Your **steamroller** is complete!

HELIPAD

Three ... two ... one ... liftoff!

1. Snap the battery holder, 5-snap wire, 4-snap wire, lamp, and motor to the base grid as shown.

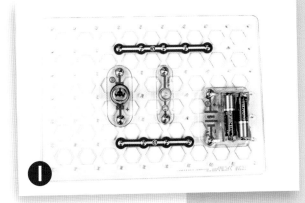

2. Use the 2-snap wires to connect the circuit as shown.

3. Use the press switch to connect the 5-snap wire to the positive end of the battery. Place the fan blade on the motor shaft.

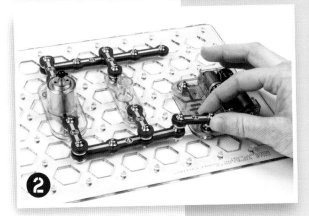

4. Press the switch to test the connection. The motor should spin the fan blade. When you release the switch, the fan blade should fly upward! If it doesn't, try switching the direction of the motor.

Continued on the next page.

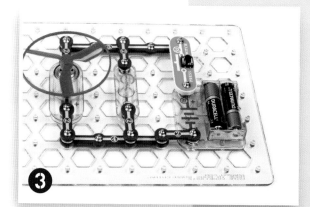

5. Open both ends of the cereal box. Cut off one large **panel**. Lay the box flat with the unprinted side facing up.

6 Draw a line on all four flaps 1 inch (2.5 cm) outside the folds. Cut along the lines.

7 Remove the fan blade from the circuit. Set the base grid on top of the unprinted side of the box. Mark the motor placement by making a dot in each of the holes surrounding the motor. Mark the lamp and the switch the same way. Make the dots as close to the light bulb and switch button as possible.

8. Set the base grid aside. Draw a circle within each set of four dots. Have an adult cut out the circles with a craft knife.

9 Place the cardboard over the base grid so the motor sticks out of its hole. Check that the cutouts above the light and the switch line up. Make the cutouts bigger if necessary. Take the cardboard off the base grid.

10. Cover your work surface with newspaper. Paint the box and let it dry. Paint a black square around the motor cutout. Let the paint dry.

11. Paint a yellow circle inside the black square. Let the paint dry.

12 **Helipads** often have a large letter H that pilots can read from the sky. Use a white paint pen to draw an "H" in the center of the yellow circle. Let the paint dry.

13 Lay the cardboard with the painted side down. Fold up the edges and tape the corners together.

14. Turn the cardboard over and set it on the base grid. Make sure the motor, lamp, and switch line up with the correct holes.

15. Decorate your helipad! Use construction paper, LEGO people, and more to make flags, bushes, or anything else you can think of.

16. Put the fan blade on the motor. Then turn on the power, press the button, and release for **liftoff**!

RUNNING STREETCAR

Wave your hand and watch this streetcar drive away!

WHAT YOU NEED

Cubelets Six Kit (battery cube, drive cube, distance cube, flashlight cube)

cardboard box • scissors

ruler • rubber band • pencil

stapler • wrapping paper

tape • construction paper

glue stick • hole punch

1. Put the battery cube on top of the drive cube.

2. Connect the distance cube to the drive cube. The **sensor** should face away from the drive cube.

3. Turn on the battery. Put your hand in front of the distance cube's sensor. The cubes should move away from your hand. If they move sideways or toward your hand, try attaching the distance cube to a different side of the drive block.

4. Connect the flashlight cube to the drive cube on the opposite side from the distance cube. The light should face away from the drive cube.

5. Make a **streetcar**. Cut a cardboard box to fit over the cubes. Make sure one long side is open. When placed over the cubes, the bottom of the box should not touch the ground. Trim the bottom of the box if necessary.

Continued on the next page.

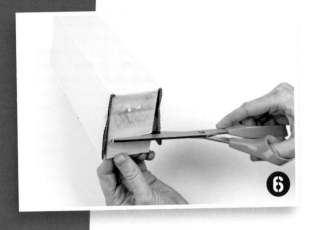

6 Cut about 1 inch (2.5 cm) off the bottom of one short side. This is the **streetcar**'s back end.

7 Cut open a rubber band. Tie one end in a knot. Tie another knot about 2 inches (5 cm) from the first knot.

8 On one long side of the box, make a mark on the bottom edge 1¾ inches (4.5 cm) from the back end of the streetcar. Staple one knot in the rubber band to the inside of the box at the mark. Staple the other knot to the other inner side of the box, directly across from the mark.

9. Cover the outside of the box with wrapping paper. Secure the paper with tape.

10 Decorate your **streetcar**! Cut windows, a door, and a windshield out of construction paper. Glue these shapes in place.

11 Punch a hole in the front of the streetcar. This is so the light can shine through.

12 Turn the streetcar upside down. Turn on the Cubelets. Turn them over and place them in the streetcar with the distance cube at the back. Stretch the rubber band over the seam between the distance cube and the drive cube.

13. Set your streetcar down. Wave your hand behind it. What happens? Your streetcar should move forward!

FLYING FISH

Watch from land as this fish takes to the sky!

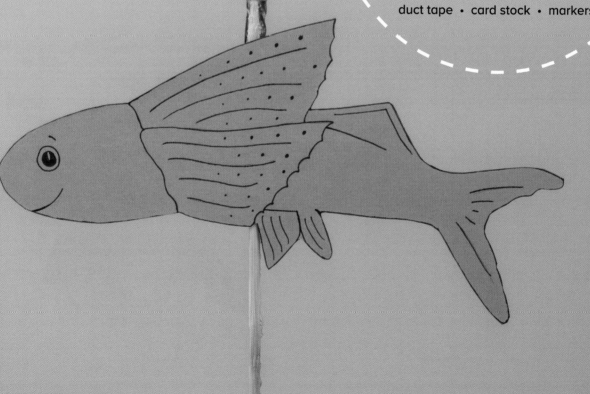

1. Cut the clip off the pen cap. Hold the cap with the top down on a block of wood. Hammer a nail through the top of the cap to make a hole.

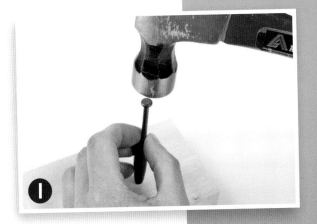

2. Hot glue the narrow end of the chopstick to the side of the pen cap.

3. Use hot glue to attach the bead to the nail hole in the pen cap. The holes should line up. Make sure glue does not fill the holes. Let the glue dry. Add more glue around the outside of this joint to make it strong. Let the glue dry.

4. Straighten the paper clips with the needle-nose pliers.

5. Hold a paper clip with the pliers 1 inch (2.5 cm) from one end. Use the pliers to make three loops in the paper clip. This creates a coil.

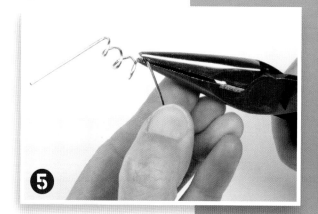

Continued on the next page.

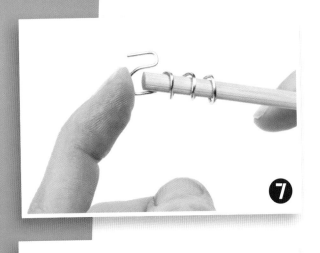

6. Cut the paper clip at the end of the coil. Use the pliers to bend the straight end into an *S*-shaped hook.

7 Fit the coil over the end of the chopstick. The hook should stick out past the end of the chopstick.

8. Turn the coil so the hook is on the same side of the chopstick as the pen cap. Hot glue the coil to the chopstick.

9 Use the pliers to make a square hook in one end of the other paper clip.

10. Put the paper clip's straight end through the hole in the **propeller**. Set the hook over the edge of the hole.

11 Hot glue the paper clip to the propeller. Center the long end of the paper clop in the hole. Hold it still until the glue sets. Do not put glue on the bottom of the propeller.

12 Put the long end of the paper clip through the bead and the pen cap. Cut the paper clip ¾ inch (2 cm) beyond the bottom of the pen cap. Make a bend in the paper clip about ½ inch (1.25 cm) from the cap.

13 Loop two rubber bands together. Loop the other two rubber bands together. Put one end of both rubber band pairs over the bent end of the paper clip on the **propeller**. Put the other ends over the hook at the bottom of the chopstick.

14. Wrap duct tape around the bottom hook to cover the sharp end of the paper clip.

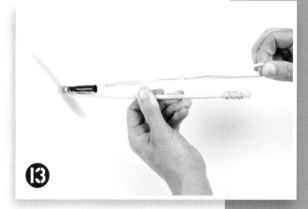

15 Cut a fish out of card stock. Decorate it with markers. Hot glue the fish to the chopstick on the side opposite the rubber bands. The top of the fish should be about 1 inch (2.5 cm) from the propeller.

16. Hold the chopstick and turn the propeller many times to wind it up. Release the propeller and then the chopstick quickly after. Watch your flying fish go!

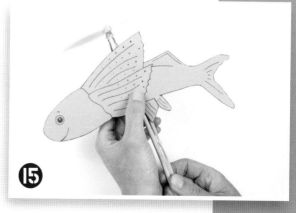

MOTORING LEGO CAR

Make a zooming electric race car!

1 Put a bushing on one end of a 6M **axle**. Add a small wheel, two 1×2 Technic bricks, and another small wheel. Put a bushing on the other end of the axle. This is the front wheel assembly.

2 Build the front of the car with LEGOs. It can look any way you want. But the area that will be between the wheels should be four **studs** wide. Attach the front wheel assembly to that area. Set the front of the car aside.

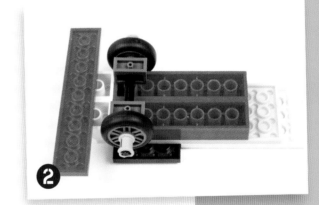

3. Put a 4M axle through an end hole of a 1×4 Technic brick. Add a 20-tooth double conical wheel and a bushing.

4 Put a 7M axle through the hole at the other end. Add a 12-tooth double conical wheel. Fit its teeth together with the 20-tooth wheel. Put both axles through a Technic 1×4 brick.

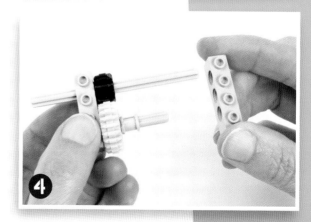

5. Add a bushing to each end of the 7M axle. Push the bushings against the other parts to hold them in place.

Continued on the next page.

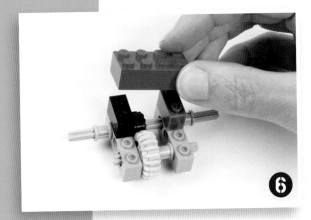

6 Put a 1×2 brick on each 1×4 Technic brick over the 7M **axle**. Connect the 1×2 bricks with a 2×4 brick.

7. Put the other 4M axle through the center hole of the short side of the Technic 3×5 angled beam. Add a bushing and a 12-tooth double conical wheel.

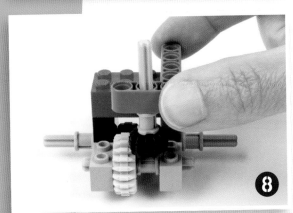

8 Turn the axle over. Fit the 12-tooth wheel together with the 20-tooth wheel. Snap the long side of the Technic beam to the 2×4 brick.

9. Put a large wheel on each end of the 7M axle. This is the back wheel assembly.

10. Form a block of LEGOs that is five bricks high. The top two bricks should be 2×4s. Connect the bottom of the block to a 2×8 brick.

11 Connect the 2×8 brick to the 2×4 brick on the back wheel assembly.

12. Connect the motorMate to the littleBits motor shaft.

13. Use the other end of the motorMate to connect the motor to the 4M **axle** on the back wheel assembly.

14. Wrap a rubber band around the littleBits motor and the block of LEGOs.

15. Use the 2×8 brick on the back wheel assembly to connect it to the front of the car.

16. Attach the battery to the power bit. Attach the power bit to the motor bit.

17. Put the battery and littleBits parts on the car. If necessary, use pieces of **adhesive foam** to hold them in place.

18. Turn on the motor and watch your race car go!

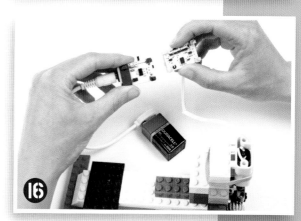

MAKERSPACE MAINTENANCE

Being a maker is not just about the finished craft. It's about communicating and **collaborating** with others as you create. The best makers also learn from their creations. They think of ways to improve them next time.

CLEANING UP

When you're done with a project, be sure to tidy up your area. Put away tools and supplies. Make sure they are organized so others can find them easily.

SAFE STORAGE

Sometimes you won't finish a project in one makerspace **session**. That's OK! Just find a safe place to store your project until you can work on it again.

MAKER FOR LIFE!

Maker project possibilities are endless. Get inspired by the materials in your makerspace. Invite new makers to your space. Check out what other makers are creating. Never stop making!

GLOSSARY

adhesive foam – craft foam that has one or more sticky sides.

axle – a bar that connects two wheels.

collaborate – to work with another person or group in order to do something or reach a goal.

dangerous – able or likely to cause harm or injury.

engineer – someone who is trained to design and build structures such as machines, cars, or roads.

gadget – a tool or device that does a specific job or task.

helipad – a special area where a helicopter can take off and land.

liftoff – a vertical takeoff by an aircraft, rocket, or missile.

panel – part of a flat surface such as a wall or screen.

permission – when a person in charge says it's okay to do something.

propeller – a device with turning blades used to move a vehicle such as an airplane or a boat.

sensor – an instrument that can detect, measure, and transmit information to a controlling device.

session – a period of time used for a specific purpose or activity.

steamroller – a steam-driven road roller.

streetcar – a vehicle that travels on tracks on city streets.

stud – a small, button-like piece projecting from a surface.

ONLINE RESOURCES

Booklinks
NONFICTION
NETWORK
FREE! ONLINE NONFICTION RESOURCES

To learn more about projects that move, visit **abdobooklinks.com**. These links are routinely monitored and updated to provide the most current information available.

INDEX